NBA CHAMPIONSHIP:

2011

ALL-TIME LEADING SCORER:

DIRK NOWITZKI (1998–PRESENT):

30,260 POINTS

(AS OF APRIL 13, 2017)

THE NBA: A HISTORY OF HOOPS

DALLAS MAVERICKS

DALLAS
8

THE NBA: A HISTORY OF HOOPS

DALLAS MAVERICKS

BY JIM WHITING

CREATIVE EDUCATION CREATIVE PAPERBACKS

Published by Creative Education
and Creative Paperbacks

P.O. Box 227, Mankato, Minnesota 56002

Creative Education and Creative Paperbacks
are imprints of The Creative Company

www.thecreativecompany.us

Design and production by Blue Design

Printed in the United States of America

Photographs by Corbis (Steve Lipofsky, John F. Rhodes/Dallas Morning News), Getty Images (Bill Baptist/NBA, Andrew D. Bernstein/NBA, Walter Bibikow, Kevork Djansezian/Getty Images Sport, Stephen Dunn, Fort Worth Star-Telegram/Tribune News Service, Jesse D. Garrabrant/NBA, Otto Greule Jr./Allsport, Glenn James/NBA, Glenn James/NBAE, Andy Lyons/Getty Images Sport, Ronald Martinez/Getty Images Sport, Fernando Medina/NBA, Tom Pennington/Getty Images Sport, Mike Powell/Getty Images Sport, Dick Raphael/NBA, Joe Robbins/Getty Images Sport, Bob Rosato/Sports Illustrated, Westend61), Newscom (Ron Jenkins/MCT, Jose Luis Villegas/ZUMA Press, Brandon Wade/MCT)

Library of Congress Cataloging-in-Publication Data

Names: Whiting, Jim, 1943- author.

Title: Dallas Mavericks / Jim Whiting.

Series: The NBA: A History of Hoops.

Includes bibliographical references and index.

Summary: This high-interest title summarizes the history of the Dallas Mavericks professional basketball team, highlighting memorable events and noteworthy players such as Dirk Nowitzki.

Identifiers: LCCN 2016054003 / ISBN 978-1-60818-841-3 (hardcover) / ISBN 978-1-62832-444-0 (pbk) / ISBN 978-1-56660-889-3 (eBook)

Subjects: LCSH: 1. Dallas Mavericks (Basketball team)—History—Juvenile literature. 2. Dallas Mavericks (Basketball team)—Biography—Juvenile literature.

Classification: LCC GV885.52.D34 W45 2017 / DDC 796.323/64097642812—dc23

CCSS: RI.4.1, 2, 3, 4; RI.5.1, 2, 4; RI.6.1, 2, 3; RF.4.3, 4; RF.5.3, 4; RH. 6-8. 4, 5, 7

First Edition HC 9 8 7 6 5 4 3 2 1

First Edition PBK 9 8 7 6 5 4 3 2 1

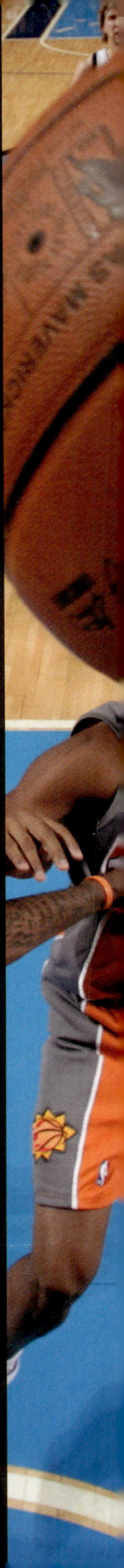

DALLAS
42
PHX

Kings
DALLAS
42

CONTENTS

Home to corporations such as AT&T and Texas Instruments, **DALLAS** is often called "Big D."

PRO HOOPS COMES TO DALLAS

The Dallas Mavericks faced the Oklahoma City Thunder in the first game of the National Basketball Association (NBA) Western

The **DALLAS MAVERICKS** beat the Thunder on their way to the 2011 NBA Finals.

Conference finals on May 17, 2011. Many people thought the Thunder's group of young talent gave them the edge. Oklahoma City featured stars Kevin Durant, James Harden, and Russell Westbrook. The Thunder bolted to an early 9-point lead. Then the Mavericks' 7-foot power forward Dirk Nowitzki took over. He sank 10 of his first 11 field goals. "I was really looking to shoot early and was able to get my rhythm after the first couple of shots," Nowitzki said. "I kept attacking, and my teammates kept feeding me and feeding me, and I was able to take advantage over some smaller players." The Thunder put six different players on Nowitzki. None was successful. Several fouled out. Sometimes they double- or triple-teamed Nowitzki. So he dished off to teammates for easy shots. In the second half, the Thunder fouled him in desperation. That didn't work, either. He made 19 straight free throws. In all, he was a perfect 24-for-24 in the game. That set an NBA playoffs record. Nowitzki finished with 48 points. The Mavs won 121–112. That win propelled them to a 4–1 series victory. They faced LeBron James and the Miami Heat in the NBA Finals. Would the Mavs clinch their first championship?

TOL
FOULS
NOWITZKI
41
BAREA
11
SPALDING
NBA TV
WESTERN
CONFERENCE
FINALS

DALLAS HORNED FROGS?

Most people in the Dallas area were pleased with the name Mavericks. Not Bill Reeves, athletic director at the nearby University of Texas at Arlington. His teams were already called the Mavericks. The school printed bumper stickers reading "Mavericks, nowhere but UTA." The NBA team's officials responded that the name came from a radio contest. UTA official John Mocek agreed the Mavericks name was a good fit for the new team. "They had the Western theme to go along with the [Major League Baseball Texas] Rangers and the [National Football League Dallas] Cowboys," he said. "But it would have been better if they were the Dallas Horned Frogs."

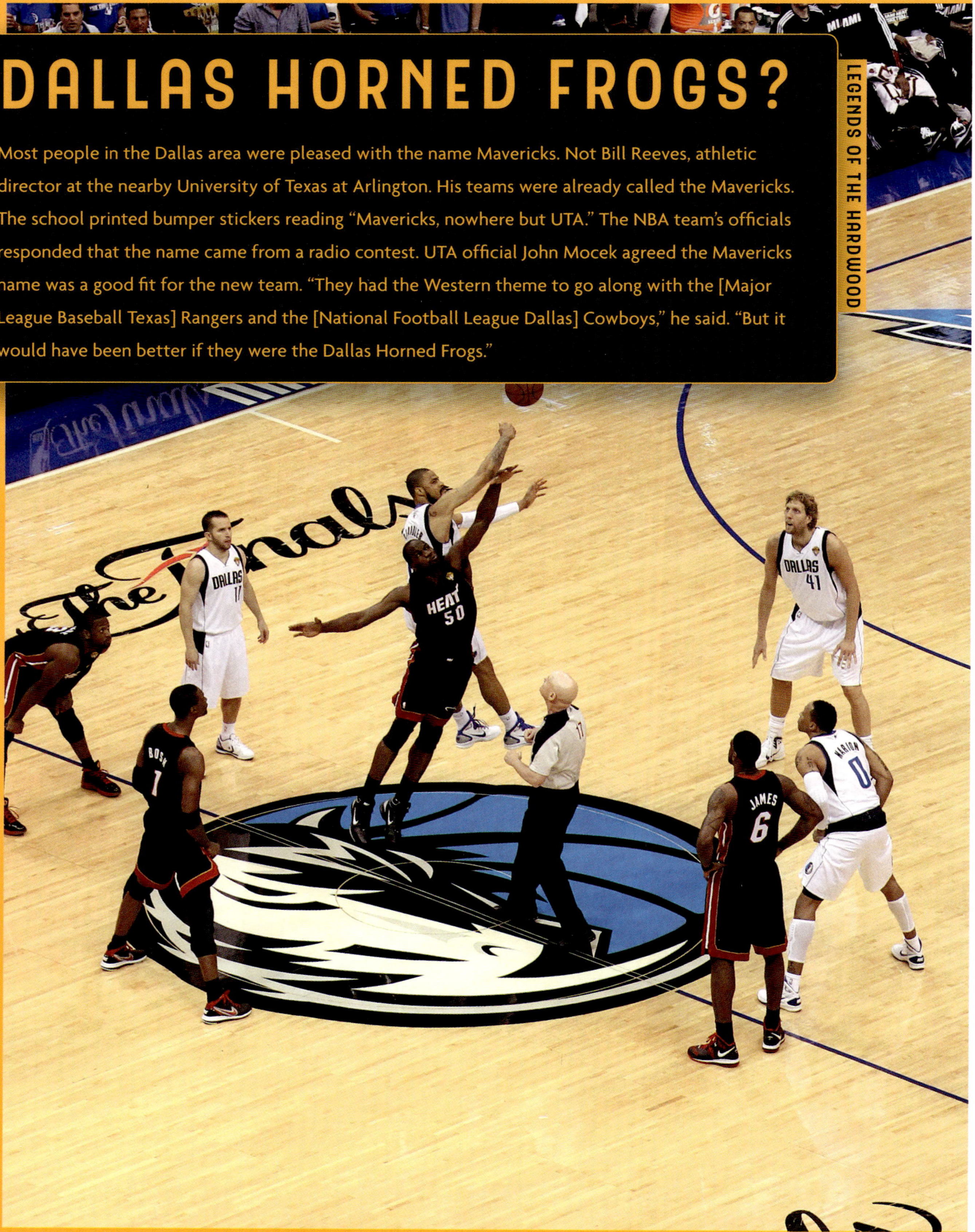

The Mavericks weren't the first professional basketball team in Dallas. The Dallas Chaparrals played in the American Basketball Association (ABA) from 1968 to 1973. The team usually made the playoffs. But it didn't attract many fans. The owners sold the team to a group of San Antonio businessmen. There, it became the Spurs. In 1978, Buffalo Braves president Norm Sonju tried to relocate his team to Dallas. The Braves went to San Diego instead. But Sonju persuaded several Dallas businessmen to form an expansion team. It began playing in the 1980–81 season. A Dallas radio station conducted a name-the-team contest. Thousands of people entered. Lead owner Don Carter narrowed the choices to Express, Mavericks, and Wranglers. He chose Mavericks, often shortened to Mavs. Forty-one people had suggested it. The team had a drawing among the group for free season tickets. Freelance writer

Point guard **BRAD DAVIS** was a reliable presence on the court for more than a decade.

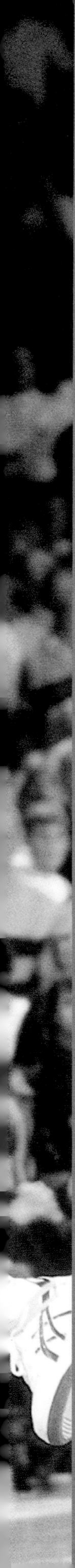

Carla Springer won the drawing. She said the nickname "represents the independent, flamboyant style of the Dallas people." The name fit well into Texas's cowboy heritage. It was also the name of the popular 1957–62 TV series *Maverick*. Star James Garner was a part-owner of the team.

The Mavericks played their first game against San Antonio. They won 103–92. But wins were rare that first season. Dallas stumbled to a 15–67 record. It was the worst in the NBA. Perhaps the best player was point guard Brad Davis. He averaged 11 points and nearly 7 assists a game.

MOVING ON UP WITH THE MAVS

Their poor record had a silver lining. The Mavs received the top pick in the 1981 NBA Draft. They chose 1980 College Player of the Year small forward/guard Mark Aguirre. They also added guard

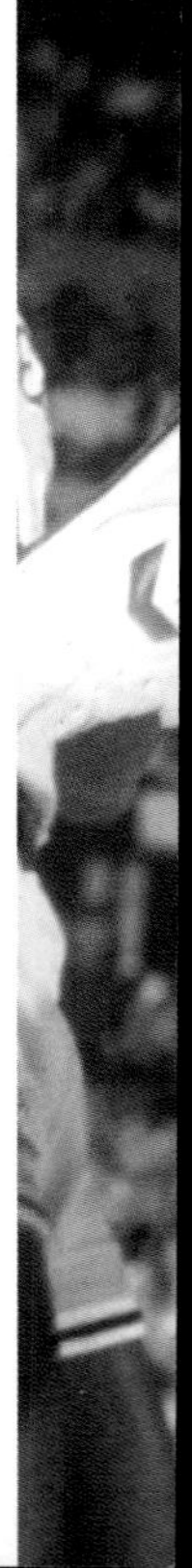

Slick-shooting **ROLANDO BLACKMAN** earned All-Star status four times with Dallas.

An elite defender, **DEREK HARPER** topped the franchise in assists and steals.

Rolando Blackman. The two helped Dallas win 28 games in 1981–82. It improved to 38 wins the following season. Things were starting to look up in the "Big D."

The Mavs added guard Derek Harper in 1983. The team's young talent produced 43 wins in 1983–84. It was the Mavs' first winning record. They made the playoffs for the first time. Dallas beat the Seattle Sonics in the first round. They fell to the Los Angeles Lakers in the Western

LEGENDS OF THE HARDWOOD

MAKING HIS MARK

MARK AGUIRRE, SMALL FORWARD, 6-FOOT-6, 1981–89

It didn't take long for Mark Aguirre to impress Dallas fans. He averaged nearly 19 points as a rookie. By 1983–84, he was averaging nearly 30 points a game. His 2,330 total points that season remains a Dallas single-season record. Aguirre became the first Mavericks player to be named to the All-Star Game. "He was a passer, he was a power player inside, and he played against bigger people," said coach John MacLeod. Unfortunately, he wasn't completely satisfied in Dallas. Aguirre often clashed with coaches and teammates. Dallas traded him to Detroit during the 1988–89 season.

With a long reach, **SAM PERKINS** had a knack for shooting over opponents' heads.

"WITH ROY ON THE FLOOR, WE TALK NBA CHAMPIONSHIP," SAID BLACKMAN. "HE BRINGS US THAT LITTLE PIECE OF MAGIC ... YOU SEE IN A PLAYER WHO IS SUPERIOR TO EVERYONE HE PLAYS AGAINST."

Conference semifinals. The Mavs did well again in the 1984 Draft. They added long-armed forward/center Sam Perkins. Dallas won 44 games that season. They couldn't get beyond the first round of the playoffs. The Mavs traded for massive James Donaldson, a 7-foot-2 center. He provided size and strength under the basket. Dallas won 44 games again. It advanced to the conference semifinals.

Everything seemed to come together in the 1986–87 season. Dallas had drafted 6-foot-11 forward/center Roy Tarpley. "With Roy on the floor, we talk NBA championship," said Blackman. "He brings us that little piece of magic ... you see in a player who is superior to everyone he plays against." The Mavs piled up 55 wins that season. They topped the Midwest Division of the Western Conference. Fans hoped that Blackman might be right. Perhaps the Mavs could win the NBA championship. They took the first step with a 151–129 blowout of the Sonics in the first game of the playoffs. But Seattle came back to take the next three games. Dallas's season was over. So was Dick Motta's time as the coach. He had led the team from the beginning.

Motta's replacement, John MacLeod, steered the team to 53 wins. Dallas beat Houston 3–1 in the first round of the playoffs. It knocked off Denver in the second round. Then the Mavs faced the Lakers in the Western Conference finals. The Lakers had a better record and the

The towering **ROY TARPLEY** averaged 10 rebounds a game during 6 Mavs seasons.

home-court advantage. That proved to be decisive. The home team won the first six games. Game 7 was in Los Angeles. Dallas trailed by just a single point at halftime. The Lakers dominated the second half. They won 117–102. Fans had high hopes for the next season. But Dallas suffered several setbacks. Tarpley was suspended. Aguirre demanded a trade. Donaldson was hurt. The Mavs stumbled to 38–44 and missed the playoffs. They rebounded in 1989–90 to win 47 games. But the Portland Trail Blazers swept them in the first round of the playoffs.

LEGENDS OF THE HARDWOOD

TRIPLE TROUBLE

SHAWN BRADLEY, CENTER, 7-FOOT-6, 1997–2005

A triple-double means a player has a double-digit tally in three categories. The five possible categories are points, rebounds, assists, steals, and blocked shots. Perhaps the most difficult triple-double is in points, rebounds, and blocked shots. Shawn Bradley ranks fourth all-time with six. In 1996, he became the first player with a blocked shot triple-double in consecutive games. He is also the leader in an unusual type of triple-double. Achieving 10 or more points, rebounds, and blocked shots—with no assists—has happened only seven times in NBA history. Bradley has done it three of those times.

DARK DAYS IN DALLAS

That was the high-water mark for nearly a decade. Dallas slid to 28 wins in 1990–91 and 22 in 1991–92. Then the bottom fell out. The Mavericks scraped by with 11 wins. It was one of the worst seasons

Forward **JAMAL MASHBURN** was a prolific scorer until he was sidelined by a knee injury.

Point guard **JASON KIDD** returned to the Mavs in 2007–08 and led them to a title in 2011.

by any team in NBA history. They were almost as bad in 1993–94, winning just 13. These poor showings enabled Dallas to have some of the top picks in the NBA Draft. It chose Jim Jackson, Jamal Mashburn, and Jason Kidd. They became known as the "Three Js." The Mavs won 36 games in 1994–95. Kidd became the first Mavericks player selected as Rookie of the Year. He shared the honor with Grant Hill of the Detroit Pistons. The next year, he started in the All-Star Game.

Unfortunately, the reign of the Three Js was short-lived. Mashburn suffered a serious knee injury in 1995. Kidd and Jackson were traded. The Mavericks won just 24 games in 1996–97. They had churned through 27 players. That broke an NBA record from the 1940s. Dallas added 7-foot-6 center Shawn Bradley and shooting guard/small forward Michael Finley. Finley led his new team in scoring, assists, and steals in 1997–98. But the Mavs dropped to just 20 wins.

Canadian import **STEVE NASH** efficiently spread the ball around the court.

Dallas hit pay dirt in the 1998 NBA Draft. It selected young German power forward Dirk Nowitzki. The team also traded for point guard Steve Nash. Basketball author Chris Ballard called it "the greatest set of draft-day trades in NBA history.... That's two MVPs [Most Valuable Players] for two bench players." In the strike-shortened 1998–99 season, the Mavs finished just 19–31. But Dallas did much better the following year. The team won 30 of its last 48 games, ending 40–42. By this time, most of the parts for success were in place. They just needed a spark to set them off.

LEGENDS OF THE HARDWOOD

SUCH A DEAL!

DIRK NOWITZKI, CENTER/POWER FORWARD, 7 FEET, 1998–PRESENT

Before the 1998 NBA Draft, German Dirk Nowitzki was an international man of mystery. "Not a lot was known about the German game at that time," said Milwaukee general manager Larry Harris. Dallas coach Don Nelson knew better. "When I saw Dirk for the first time, he was the greatest 17- or 18-year-old or whatever he was that I'd ever witnessed," he said. The Mavericks had the sixth pick in the 1998 Draft. They could have taken Nowitzki then. Instead, they cut a deal with the Milwaukee Bucks. The Bucks needed a bruising big man. They had their eyes on Robert "Tractor" Traylor. So the Mavs drafted Traylor. The Bucks took Nowitzki. Then they swapped.

High-scoring swingman **MICHAEL FINLEY** helped Dallas reach the playoffs five times.

WITH A LITTLE EFFORT

In 2000, 42-year-old tech billionaire Mark Cuban bought the team. The coaching staff feared the worst. "Dirk [Nowitzki] hadn't kicked in, [Steve] Nash couldn't make a jump shot, so we literally went out and

Dallas's all-time leading scorer, **DIRK NOWITZKI**, could shoot from any angle.

thought we were going to be fired the next day when we showed up," said assistant coach Donnie Nelson. His father Don was the team's head coach. New owners often released the current coaching and front office staffs. "Then the next day Mark walks in Nellie's [Don Nelson's] office in a T-shirt, jeans, and his patented tennis shoes. And Nellie leans over to me and he goes, 'Son, I think we might have a chance with this one.'"

Cuban made it clear that he wouldn't accept mediocrity with the Mavericks. He recognized that Nelson knew more than he did. He didn't interfere with him. Cuban showed his willingness to pay top dollar for players. He also treated his players much better than they had been accustomed to. "He bought us a new plane, he got us a new arena, we started staying in nice hotels, we started to have food after games and after practices, and he just put Dallas basketball back on the map," Nowitzki said. Cuban became known for doing many offbeat things. He served as a celebrity bartender. He worked the counter at a Dairy Queen. He even played basketball with the Harlem Globetrotters.

His efforts paid off. Nash directed the offense. All-Star forward Juwan Howard joined Nowitzki and Finley. The high-powered Mavs went 53–29 in 2000–01. It was their first winning record in a decade. Dallas lost in the conference semifinals that year and the next. The team soon became a melting pot of players from other countries. Nowitzki

AVERICKS
41
LIOTT
32

MAVS ON THE MAP

LEGENDS OF THE HARDWOOD

MARK CUBAN, OWNER, 2000–PRESENT

Many people credit Mark Cuban with the rise of the Mavericks. In its first 20 years, Dallas won just 40 percent of its games. "Nobody was paying attention to the Mavericks really and then Mark took over," said forward Dirk Nowitzki. "He's turned that town [Dallas] around," added Sacramento Kings co-owner Joe Maloof. Unlike many NBA owners, Cuban likes to wear a Mavs jersey and sit next to fans. He is also a noted television personality. He has appeared on the ABC *Shark Tank* series since 2010. He is one of several panelists who consider investing in products inventors present to them.

was German. Nash was from Canada. Three other players were foreign: center Wang Zhizhi (China), forward Eduardo Najera (Mexico) and guard Tariq Abdul-Wahad (France). "Having players that are national heroes adds quite a bit to the team," Cuban said. Dallas surged to 60 wins in 2002–03. In an "All-Dallas" conference finals, the Spurs (formerly Dallas Chaparrals) defeated the Mavericks. "It was a matter of them turning their gear up a level, and we couldn't get any higher," explained Coach Nelson. "That was the end of it."

It was hardly the end of Dallas's success. The Mavericks won "only" 52 games in 2003–04 and lost in the first round of the playoffs. Dallas upped the victory total to 58 in 2004–05. Nelson stunned the team by stepping down late in the season. Assistant coach Avery Johnson replaced him. "I see a little slippage as a team," Nelson said. "The team is just responding better to Avery at this point." Dallas powered back to 60 wins the following season. One key was veteran guard Jason Terry. He averaged 17 points a game. The Mavs charged through the first three rounds of the playoffs. They met Shaquille O'Neal and the Miami Heat in the NBA Finals. Dallas felt good about its chances. It had defeated the Heat in both regular-season matches. The Mavs trampled them in the first two games. But Miami won the next four. Three of those Dallas losses were by three points or fewer.

TAKING THE TITLE

The near miss made Dallas fans eagerly anticipate the following season. The Mavs didn't disappoint. They surged to 67 wins. It was the top record in the NBA. It was also a tie for the sixth-

Lightning-fast point guard **DEVIN HARRIS** led Dallas to the 2006 Finals against the Heat.

During his brief time in Dallas, forward **TIM THOMAS** provided a veteran presence.

"IF THERE WAS ONE GUY WHO KNEW HOW TO DEFEND DIRK [NOWITZKI], IT WAS THE GUY COACHING THE OTHER TEAM," CUBAN SAID. NOWITZKI AGREED. "I THINK NELLIE HAD OBVIOUSLY THE EXACT BLUEPRINT ON HOW TO PLAY US."

best record in NBA history. The Mavs faced the Golden State Warriors in the playoffs. The Warriors sneaked into the playoffs with a 42–40 record. Yet Golden State won the series four games to two. It became the first eighth seed to knock off the top seed in a best-of-seven series. One reason for the shocking upset may have been the Warriors' coach, Don Nelson. "If there was one guy who knew how to defend Dirk [Nowitzki], it was the guy coaching the other team," Cuban said. Nowitzki agreed. "I think Nellie had obviously the exact blueprint on how to play us," he said.

Dallas continued to play well in the next three seasons. The Mavericks won at least 50 games each time. But they suffered early playoff defeats. Before the 2010–11 season, Dallas added 7-foot-1 center Tyson Chandler. He was named to the NBA All-Defensive team. Dallas won 57 games. Fans were encouraged when the Mavs beat the Trail Blazers 4–2 in the first round of the playoffs.

LEGENDS OF THE HARDWOOD

BACKING OUT

In the summer of 2015, Los Angeles Clippers center DeAndre Jordan was a free agent. He verbally agreed to a four-year contract with the Mavericks. Five days later, he said he would rejoin the Clippers. Mavericks officials visited his home. He refused to let them in. The free agency period was nearly over. The best remaining centers had signed with other teams. Dallas had to take what was left. The Mavericks hosted the Clippers on November 11. Fans booed Jordan. They cheered his missed shots. One fan held up a sign that said, “The only thing worse than Jordan’s word is his free throw percentage.”

> "THIS IS A TRUE TEAM," SAID COACH RICK CARLISLE. "WE DON'T RUN FAST OR JUMP HIGH. [BUT] THESE GUYS HAD EACH OTHER'S BACKS. WE PLAYED THE RIGHT WAY."

Nearly all of them wore "The Time Is Now" T-shirts. Dallas swept the Lakers in the second round. The Mavs silenced the Oklahoma City Thunder in the conference finals. They arrived at the NBA Finals to face the Miami Heat. After being down two games to one, Dallas won the next three. The Mavericks had their first NBA title! Nowitzki was named series MVP. "This is a true team," said coach Rick Carlisle. "We don't run fast or jump high. [But] these guys had each other's backs. We played the right way.... This is a phenomenal thing for the city of Dallas."

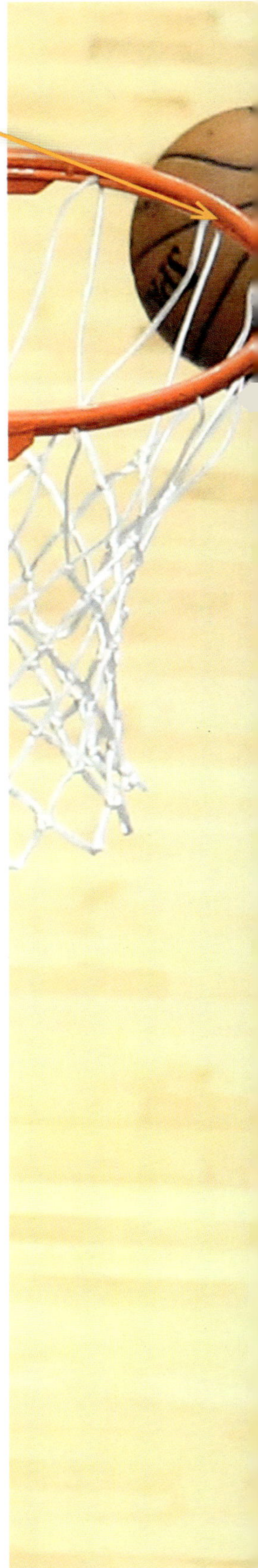

Defensive-minded guard **WESLEY MATTHEWS** worked tirelessly on and off the court.

In 2011, forward **SHAWN MARION** became just the fifth NBA player to record 1,500 steals and 1,000 blocked shots.

Dallas fans hoped for a repeat championship. But labor difficulties delayed the start of the 2011–12 season. Dallas went 36–30. The Oklahoma City Thunder swept the Mavs in the first round of the playoffs. With 41 wins the following season, the Mavericks missed the playoffs. The next two seasons had virtually identical win totals, but the Mavs still could not advance in the playoffs. Dallas wanted to bolster the backcourt for 2015–16. It brought in shooting guard Wesley Matthews.

DALLAS
23
LEE

Dallas bolstered its lineup with versatile forward **DWIGHT POWELL** in 2014–15.

He was Portland's all-time leader in three-pointers. Point guard Deron Williams also became a Mav. He played on two gold-medal-winning Olympics teams. The Mavs made the playoffs. But the Thunder boxed them out in the first round. Dallas suffered a nine-game falloff in 2016–17, finishing just 33–49. It was the Mavs' first losing season since 1998–99. The only excitement as the season ended came when longtime Dallas Cowboys cuarterback Tony Romo joined the team for a pregame shoot-around, and Nowitzki moved into sixth place in the league's career scoring list. The late-season trade for center/power forward Nerlens Noel gave hope moving forward.

The Mavericks have been one of the NBA's most consistent teams since the turn of the century. Fans feel confident that their team will always be in the playoffs. They hope that another championship banner will soon be raised in American Airlines Arena.

SELECTED BIBLIOGRAPHY

Ballard, Chris. *The Art of a Beautiful Game: The Thinking Fan's Tour of the NBA*. New York: Simon & Schuster, 2010.

Hubbard, Jan, ed. *The Official NBA Basketball Encyclopedia*. 3rd edition. New York: Doubleday, 2000.

NBA.com. "Dallas Mavericks." http://www.mavs.com/.

Scout.com. "Dallas Mavericks NBA Basketball." http://www.scout.com/nba/mavericks/.

Simmons, Bill. *The Book of Basketball: The NBA According to the Sports Guy*. New York: Ballantine, 2009.

Sports Illustrated. *Sports Illustrated Basketball's Greatest*. New York: Sports Illustrated, 2014.

WEBSITES

DUCKSTERS BASKETBALL: NBA

http://www.ducksters.com/sports/national_basketball_association.php

Learn more about NBA history, rules, positions, strategy, drills, and other topics.

JR. NBA

http://jr.nba.com/

This kids site has games, videos, game results, team and player information, statistics, and more.

Note: Every effort has been made to ensure that any websites listed above were active at the time of publication. However, because of the nature of the Internet, it is impossible to guarantee that these sites will remain active indefinitely or that their contents will not be altered.

INDEX